SAYINGS and PHRASES

That's the Last Straw!

(And Other Weird Things We Say)

written by Cynthia Amoroso ★ illustrated by Mernie Gallagher-Cole

ABOUT THE AUTHOR

As a high school English teacher and as an elementary teacher, Cynthia Amoroso has shared her love of language with students. She has always been fascinated with idioms and figures of speech. Today Cynthia is a school district administrator in Minnesota. She has two daughters who also share her love of language through reading, writing, and talking!

ABOUT THE ILLUSTRATOR

Mernie Gallagher-Cole lives in Pennsylvania with her husband and two children. She uses sayings and phrases like the ones in this book every day. She has illustrated many children's books, including *Messy Molly* and *Día De Los Muertos* for The Child's World®.

The Child's World®

Published by The Child's World®
1980 Lookout Drive • Mankato, MN 56003-1705
800-599-READ • www.childsworld.com

ACKNOWLEDGMENTS
The Child's World®: Mary Berendes,
Publishing Director

The Design Lab: Kathleen Petelinsek,
Design and Page Production

**LIBRARY OF CONGRESS
CATALOGING-IN-PUBLICATION DATA**
Amoroso, Cynthia.
 That's the last straw!: (and other weird things we
say) / by Cynthia Amoroso; Illustrated by Mernie
Gallagher-Cole.
   p. cm.
 ISBN 978-1-60954-230-6 (library bound: alk. paper)
1. English language—Idioms—Juvenile literature.
2. Figures of speech—Juvenile literature. 3. Clichés—
Juvenile literature. I. Gallagher-Cole, Mernie. II. Title.
 PE1460.A59 2011
 428.1—dc22   2010042741

Printed in the United States of America
Mankato, MN
December, 2010
PA02067

People use idioms *(ID-ee-umz) every day. These are sayings and phrases with meanings that are different from the actual words. Some idioms seem silly. Many of them don't make much sense . . . at first.*

This book will help you understand some of the most common idioms. It will tell you how you might hear a saying or phrase. It will tell you what the saying really means. All of these sayings and short phrases—even the silly ones—are an important part of our language!

TABLE *of* CONTENTS

Along for the ride

"Let's have burgers for dinner!" voted Erika as she and her family entered the food court.

"No, let's have pizza!" said Tara.

"I'd rather have tacos," said their brother Thomas.

"How about if we let Mom choose?" Erika asked. "Mom, what should we eat?"

"Don't worry about me," Mom replied. "I had a late lunch, so I'm not hungry. I'm just along for the ride."

MEANING: To do something just to be with the group

Backseat driver

Annie was studying to get her driver's license. She was nervous about passing the test. Whenever she rode in a car, she watched the traffic closely. She also reacted to any dangers she saw.

"Look out!" she cried for the third time. "Grandma, that car is going to turn."

"I see it," Grandma answered with a chuckle. "I saw the last one, too. I'm glad you're paying attention, dear, but I don't really need a backseat driver."

MEANING: A passenger in a car who tells the driver what to do

5

Blow your own horn

"I won! I won!" shouted Kelly as she ran into the kitchen. She had trained for the race for two months. She was so happy to have her first-place medal.

"That's wonderful!" said Aunt Kate.

"Thanks," said Kelly. "I don't mean to blow my own horn, but I was definitely the fastest girl there!"

MEANING: To tell others when you do something well; to brag about yourself

By leaps and bounds

Brody spent the weekend learning to water ski. It took him a whole day just to learn to stand up! Now he wanted to see how far he could go.

Uncle Jim started the motor. As the rope tightened, Brody bent his knees and held on. Up he went! Uncle Jim made a loop all the way around the lake and brought Brody back to shore.

"That was great, Brody!" said Uncle Jim. "You're improving by leaps and bounds!"

MEANING: When something happens quickly

Calm before the storm

Bridget's school was hosting a big gymnastics meet. Bridget and her teammates helped their coaches get everything ready. Now Bridget and Ms. Adams were checking the list for the last time. The rest of the team had already gone home.

"Wow!" said Bridget. "The gym seems really quiet."

"Doesn't it?" replied Ms. Adams with a grin. "But just wait until tomorrow morning, when all the teams arrive! This is just the calm before the storm."

MEANING: A time that seems unusually quiet, especially when trouble is coming

Clear the air

Lucy and Mia were best friends, but they hadn't spoken for a week. They'd had an argument and were still angry.

Finally, Lucy called Mia on the phone. They talked about what had happened and apologized to each other.

Afterward, Lucy was talking with her mom. "I'm so glad Mia and I are friends again!" she exclaimed.

"I thought it wouldn't take long," said Mom. "You just needed to clear the air."

MEANING: To talk things out and make sure everyone understands a situation; to get rid of problems that have complicated a situation

Every cloud has a silver lining

"Today was so much fun!" said Ava. She and her older sister spent the day at the mall. They went shopping and ate lunch at a new restaurant. They even went to a movie.

"I was really upset this morning when I saw that it was raining," said Ava. "I really wanted to go to the water park. But I think we had more fun at the mall!"

"I think so, too," said her sister. "Every cloud has a silver lining."

MEANING: Something good or happy can result from something that doesn't go the way you want

Flew the coop

Christopher was at his Uncle Tim's farm, helping his uncle round up the goats. It was time to bring them into the barn.

"Uncle Tim, aren't there supposed to be twenty-two goats?" asked Christopher.

"Yes," replied Uncle Tim. "How many did you count?"

"Only twenty-one," said Christopher. "Is the gate open? I think somebody flew the coop!"

MEANING: Escaped

Get the scoop

Shaun and his brother Aiden were really excited. The city was putting in a new swimming pool. It looked like it was almost ready, but when would it open? The boys were eager to find out.

"Why don't you call the Parks Department?" suggested their Dad.

"Good idea!" said Shaun as he ran for the phone. Soon he came back, waving a piece of paper. "Okay, I got the scoop!" he said. "It opens next Friday."

MEANING: To get information

Give you the shirt off his back

Bailey and her classmates were collecting donations for people who had lost their homes in a flood. Bailey came back from a neighbor's house dragging two big sacks.

"Mr. Wallace really gave us a lot!" she exclaimed. "He donated some new clothes and lots of food. That was really nice of him."

"He's a kind and generous man," Dad agreed. "He'd give you the shirt right off his back."

MEANING: To do anything possible to help another person; to be unselfish in giving to another person

Hands down

Aimee and her dad loved ice cream. Every Saturday, they walked to the little sundae shop down the street. The owners made their own ice cream.

"What do you think is their best flavor?" asked Dad as they walked along.

"Oh, that's easy!" said Aimee. "Caramel swirl is good, but chocolate chunk is the winner, hands down!"

MEANING: When something or somebody wins easily; when a choice is made without any doubt

Hear a pin drop

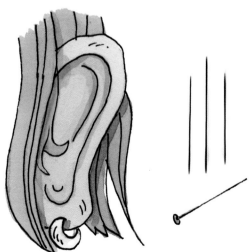

Josef had just won the citywide spelling bee.

"Great job!" said Mr. Ellis, his English teacher. "We were all worried on that last one!"

"We sure were," said Josef's dad. "You spelled the first few letters right away, but then you stopped for such a long time."

"The crowd got so quiet," said Mr. Ellis, "that you could hear a pin drop."

MEANING: To be completely silent; to have no noise at all

Let sleeping dogs lie

"Mom," asked Adrienne, "isn't Jason's family good friends with the Millers? They don't seem to do much together anymore."

"No, they don't," replied Mom. "They had a disagreement last year. They still get along, but they don't spend much time with each other."

"That's too bad," said Adrienne. "Maybe somebody should talk to them about it."

"I don't think that would help," answered Mom. "Sometimes it's better to let sleeping dogs lie."

MEANING: Leave well enough alone; don't stir up a situation that might be troublesome

A little bird told me

Kara's birthday had been a lot of fun. She had a wonderful birthday dinner with her family. Her present was a necklace she had seen at a craft fair and really liked.

"This was the necklace I really wanted! You weren't even there!" she exclaimed to her mom. "How did you know?"

"Oh, a little bird told me," Mom said, with a sly look at Grandma.

MEANING: I have some information, but I'm not saying where I got it

Muddy the waters

Lisa's family was going to a meeting at City Hall. Some people were trying to convince the city to start a dog park where dogs could play. Lisa and her parents were discussing what they should say.

Suddenly Lisa's younger brother said, "I think they should have a skate park, too. Let's ask them about that."

"I think we'd better wait," said Dad. "Let's not muddy the waters. Let's just focus on the dog park."

MEANING: To confuse a situation; to make trouble; to make things more complicated

Nose for trouble

"Dad, what were you and Uncle Pete like when you were kids?" asked Jason.

"Well," said Dad, "Pete's a couple of years older than me. I was pretty good when I was little. That's partly because I was scared to do some of the things Uncle Pete did!"

"Did he do things he wasn't supposed to?" Jason asked.

"He sure did," said Dad with a chuckle. "Our mom said he had a nose for trouble!"

MEANING: To be in trouble often; to find yourself in a bad situation when you don't intend to be

Old hat

Monday was the first day of school, and Travis was excited.
"Do you remember your bus number?" asked Mom as she helped
him lay out his clothes.

"Yup! It's 131. I can't wait!"

"Really?" said Mom. "That's great! Last year you were scared to
ride the bus. This year it's old hat."

**MEANING: To do something you have done many
times before; to have experience doing something**

One-hit wonder

Mom and Dad were listening to their favorite radio station as they drove to the store. Sonia really liked some of these old songs! It was fun when her parents sang along.

"I remember this one," said Mom as a new song started. "I haven't heard it in years."

"Do you remember who sings it? asked Dad.

"No," Mom replied. "I can't remember his name. He was a one-hit wonder."

MEANING: To be successful at something only one time

Pain in the neck

Jared and his aunt and uncle were camping. It rained for two days, but the sun had finally come out. Now Aunt Kim and Uncle John were showing Jared how to spread everything out to dry.

"This really takes a long time!" Jared complained.

"I know," Aunt Kim replied. "It's a pain in the neck. But it's worth it to have a dry sleeping bag the next night!"

MEANING: Something that is a hassle; something you don't like to do

Play your cards right

Maria and her sister were helping their parents with yard work.

"You know," Maria said to her dad, "we're getting so much done. You should take us out for pizza and a movie tonight!"

"Well, I don't know about that," said Dad. "We all have to get up pretty early tomorrow. But if you play your cards right, maybe we can go for ice cream after dinner."

MEANING: To do things well; to do things right; to plan well

Pull the wool over his eyes

A new member of the drama club volunteered to be in charge of costumes. Now Shaundra and her friend Britta were looking over the first samples.

"Uh-oh," said Shaundra. "These won't work at all. They're not even from the right time period. I thought she knew what she was doing!"

"She said she had a lot of experience at her last school," Britta replied. "She really pulled the wool over everyone's eyes!"

MEANING: To fool someone; to make someone believe something that is not true

19

Quit bellyaching

Hayley loved hearing about when her grandma had been little. Things were so different then! Grandma had grown up on a farm, which was very different from Hayley's city life.

"You really did chores every morning before you went to school?" Hayley asked. "That must have been cold in the winter!"

"It certainly was," said Grandma with a grin. "When we complained about it, our dad just told us to quit bellyaching and get to work!"

MEANING: To stop complaining or whining

Rub it in

Noah was growing a lot this year. His Aunt Charlotte wasn't very tall. Noah hadn't seen her for a few months, and he had grown a lot— almost an inch!

"Hey, Aunt Charlotte!" said Noah with a grin when she arrived. "I can see right over your head."

"I always knew you'd be taller than me someday," she replied, laughing, "but don't rub it in!"

MEANING: To make someone feel badly because they don't have something you do; to make a big deal out of something

Straight from the horse's mouth

Alex and his baseball teammates were confused. One schedule said practice was Monday after school. Another schedule said practice was Tuesday instead.

"Do you know which one is right?" Alex asked his teammates.

The boys all said "No" or shook their heads.

Just then the catcher came running up. "This is straight from the horse's mouth," he said. "Coach Hastings says practice is on Tuesday."

MEANING: To get information directly from the person who would know

That's the last straw

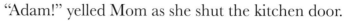

"Adam!" yelled Mom as she shut the kitchen door.

"He's not here," answered Dad. "I haven't seen him for a while. What's wrong?"

"I gave him three chores to do, and he hasn't done them," said Mom. "Then I went into the garage, and found his baseball equipment everywhere. That's the last straw!" she exclaimed.

MEANING: When several things happen that bother you, and finally you can't stand it anymore

We'll cross that bridge when we come to it

Grace was excited to have her first lawn-mowing job. "Here's how much I'll make every week," she said to her dad. "By the end of the summer, I'll have enough money to buy my own computer!"

"That's great!" said Dad.

"But what kind should I get?" asked Grace. "There are so many choices!"

"Don't worry about that right now," Dad answered. "We'll cross that bridge when we come to it."

MEANING: To not worry about something before you have to; to pay attention to what you are doing now rather than thinking about things too far into the future

Wouldn't touch it with a ten-foot pole

Jana and her friend Eve were looking over the script for a new play. It was a comedy written by some of their classmates.

"Did you read the lines Mrs. Wibble is supposed to say in Act 1?" asked Eve. "Those jokes are terrible!"

"I know!" agreed Jana. "I wouldn't touch Mrs. Wibble's role with a ten-foot pole!"

MEANING: To show distaste for something dangerous or unpleasant